The
Lord's Supper...
Let's Get Ready!

by Laurie Donahue
and Paul Phillipps
Illustrations by Scott Palmer

ISBN   0-9718306-6-5
ISBN   978-0-9718306-6-0

Published by LifeSong Publishers
P.O. Box 183, Somis, CA 93066-0183
(805) 655-5644
www.lifesongpublishers.com

Illustrations by Scott Palmer
Cover art by Ed Olson
Cover design by Design Point DesignPoint

The Lord's Supper...
Let's Get Ready!

Dear Parents,

One of my greatest joys as a pastor is to lead believers regularly in the Lord's Supper. Our Lord Jesus Christ Himself gave us this remembrance so that He is ever on our minds and the focus of our corporate worship always. In particular, He desires that we never lose sight of the cross where He took our sins upon Himself, dying in our place as the just for the unjust. He did this in order that He might bring us into a joyous relationship with the Father through faith. This is what Christianity is all about, knowing the only true God, and Jesus Christ whom He sent (John 17:3).

The apostle Paul tells us in 1 Corinthians 11 that when we partake of the elements in the Lord's Supper, we are not only remembering Christ, but specifically proclaiming His death until He comes (1 Cor. 11:26). Therefore, though the Lord's Supper is a celebration of the glorious gospel ("good news") of Jesus Christ, it is also to be a time for solemn reflection. To participate in the Lord's Supper therefore includes some important prerequisites from us.

First, of course, we must understand the significance of the Lord's Supper. Parents, this is one of the primary reasons for which we wrote this workbook. We want to assist you in your role of bringing up your children (I have nine myself!) in the discipline and instruction of the Lord (Eph. 6:4). We hope and pray that this tool will help you clarify the meaning of the Lord's Supper to your precious child. If your child does not yet know Christ, this will also provide you an occasion to explain how to become a Christian.

Secondly, the Lord's Supper is to be a time of self-examination. As the Lord brings our sins to mind, we must confess them to Him and forsake them, finding His promised forgiveness and cleansing (1 John 1:9). Your son or daughter will be encouraged in this process as he or she works through *The Lord's Supper...Let's Get Ready!* Overall, we are praying that this study will deepen relationships with Christ, and bring greater significance to the Lord's Supper when it is received. Parents, we are asking the Lord to do an eternal work in your child's heart through this book!

Because of His amazing grace through Christ,
Paul
2 Cor. 4:5

Dear Students,

I am so glad that you are going to be studying through this workbook about the Lord's Supper. It shows that you have an interest in knowing God better. There is so much to know about Him, and this is a really good time in your life to get out your "magnifying glass" and start looking deeper into the Bible. *The Lord's Supper... Let's Get Ready!* will help you know more about Jesus, help you trust Him more, and deepen your relationship with Him.

This study covers a long period of time in the Bible. It takes us all the way back to Adam and Eve in the Garden of Eden and shows how God's love for His children was great from the beginning. If you look closely, you can see how God provided for and rescued His people throughout the Bible. He saved them from the very beginning and still saves those who trust Him today. As you go through this study, look for all the places that God loved and rescued His people.

Whether communion is new to you or you are already receiving it, my prayer is that through your study of *The Lord's Supper... Let's Get Ready!,* it will become more meaningful to you. Communion is a gift that will become much more precious as you understand what it is and put it into practice.

This study presumes that you already have a relationship with God through Jesus Christ. Many of you may have been through the book *God... Should I Be Baptized?* and received Jesus as Lord and Savior then. But if you are not sure, it is NOT too late! This is a good time to talk to someone-- like a parent, pastor or Sunday School teacher-- who knows God and can help and guide you.

I am praying that *The Lord's Supper... Let's Get Ready!* will help you know more about Jesus Christ, help you trust Him more and make your relationship deeper. May you better understand the great sacrifice of Jesus' life for you. I am praying that the Lord's Supper will have new meaning as you receive it. May you grow through this study and continue to grow after it is finished.

God Bless!!
Laurie

Session 1
The Beginnings

Where Does The Lord's Supper Come From?

The Beginnings

The Lord's Supper... You have probably seen others in your church receive the Lord's Supper or you may have even received it yourself. Has it seemed confusing or complicated... something that is just for adults. Or have you thought it was only a chance to quiet the morning hunger pangs for those who skipped breakfast? Well, I am so glad you are here, because that is not what it is meant to be. God has given to us, to me and to YOU, this wonderful gift for some very special reasons.

We are going to spend a few weeks talking about the Lord's Supper and looking into God's Word to see what it means for you!

The Lord's Supper is sometimes called "communion." The word "communion" originally comes from the Greek "koinonia" which means "having in common, fellowship or sharing." We will use the terms "the Lord's Supper" and "Communion" to mean the same.

Read 1 Corinthians 10:16.

The cup of blessing which we bless, is it not the communion of the blood of Christ? The bread which we break, is it not the communion of the body of Christ? 1 Corinthians 10:16 NKJV

Read the same verse in a different version of the Bible.

Is not the cup of blessing which we bless a sharing in the blood of Christ? Is not the bread which we break a sharing in the body of Christ?
1 Corinthians 10:16 NASB

In what do these verses say we are sharing ?

_____

We will learn in these four sessions what this means as well as many other important things about the gift of communion that God has given to us.

Back To The Beginning

What if I asked you, "When did the Lord's Supper begin?" Those of you who are pretty familiar with the Bible would answer, "In the New Testament, because that is where Jesus gave the first communion." And you are correct! But to completely understand the Lord's

Supper, would you believe that we have to go back to the very first book in the Bible? That is right, way back to the book of Genesis. That is where we see sin enter the world and God promised Jesus as our solution.

Read Genesis 3:1-15 in your Bible. Notice how Adam and Eve disobeyed God. God had created a perfect world, with only one rule. Satan tempted Adam and Eve and they chose to disobey.

Read Romans 5:12.

Therefore, just as sin entered the world through one man, and death through sin, and in this way death came to all men, because all sinned... Romans 5:12

SIN— the big and very bad problem!

What 2 things entered the world because of Adam and Eve's disobedience?

_____ and _____

Sin and death entered the world, which is a big, big problem for us!

...for all have sinned and fall short of the glory of God. Romans 3:23

According to Romans 3:23, who sins, or disobeys, God?

_____

Sin separates us all from God.

According to Romans 6:23, what is the result of sin?

For the wages of sin is death, Romans 6:23

_____

What kind of death is this verse talking about?_____

Yes, this verse is talking about spiritual death, that is being eternally separated from God.

How does knowing that your sin separates you from God make you feel? _____

Read Isaiah 64:6.

> **All of us have become like one who is unclean, and all our righteous acts are like filthy rags; we all shrivel up like a leaf, and like the wind our sins sweep us away. Isaiah 64:6**

What does this say about the "good" things you do?

_____

Will the "good" things you do earn God's favor? Can you do anything on your own to have a right relationship with God?

_____

This sounds really discouraging. Being separated from God who gives us our life and everything in it, is a very lonely situation.

But read on!!...

V God's Victory Plan

God loves us so much that He doesn't want to see us die and be separated from Him. He wants us to live forever with Him. What did God do to solve our sin problem?

Read 1 John 4:10.

This is love: not that we loved God, but that he loved us and sent his Son as an atoning sacrifice for our sins.   1 John 4:10

Jesus atoned for our sins when He obeyed the law perfectly for us, since we could not and then took our punishment for us on the cross. When he died on the cross, He made us "at-one" with God when we place our faith in Him.

Read Ephesians 2:8-9.

For it is by grace you have been saved, through faith—and this not from yourselves, it is the gift of God— not by works, so that no one can boast. Ephesians 2:8-9

How does this verse describe grace?_____

_____

But let's stop for just a minute. Before we go on, we need to be certain we are all on the same track. Let's be sure you understand that our sin separates us from God and it results in spiritual death. God provided a solution for us when He sent Jesus to take our punishment on Himself when He died on the cross. If you have not received Jesus Christ as Lord and Savior, this is the time to talk about it with your teacher before we go any further. Discuss it now during class time or at the very latest right after class. Be sure you know you share in God's victory!*

God gave us the promise that Jesus would take our place on the cross way back in the Old Testament! Read Isaiah 53:5.

> **But he was pierced for our transgressions, he was crushed for our iniquities; the punishment that brought us peace was upon him, and by his wounds we are healed. Isaiah 53:5**

At that point, all the people that were born before Jesus could look forward to the fact that a Savior would die in their place to rescue them. All of the people that have lived since Jesus can look back to Jesus' death and resurrection. But both are saved by believing God's promise that Jesus takes their place on the cross, dies and rises again.

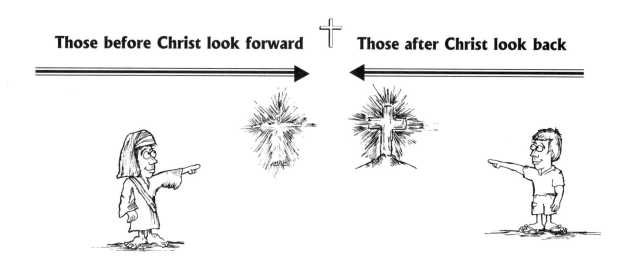

Those before Christ look forward ✝ **Those after Christ look back**

*Note to Teacher: See "God... Should I Be Baptized"- Session 2

We who live now have a definite advantage. We have seen how God carried out His victory plan. Those who lived before Jesus did not see exactly how it would happen. So God gave them some special laws and symbols to help them understand.

Passover was an event in Jewish history that helps us understand more about God's love for us and His plan for us. You may have Jewish friends who have talked about Passover. It has an important meaning for us as Christians, too. Let's look a little more closely at what happened many years ago.

God's People And Passover

Although Passover is a Jewish celebration, it has meaning for us

 because Jesus gave the first communion, also known as "the Last Supper" to His disciples during Passover.

Passover was very important to the Israelites because it reminded them of how God had rescued them from slavery. It is important to us because it is a symbol of what Christ has done for us.

Let's review the wonderful story of how God delivered His people who were prisoners in Egypt.

The Passover Story

The Egyptian Pharaoh made slaves of God's people, the Israelites, for many years. But God promised Moses that He would rescue them as we read in Exodus 3:16,17.

"Go, assemble the elders of Israel and say to them, 'The LORD, the God of your fathers-- the God of Abraham, Isaac and Jacob-- appeared to me and said: I have watched over you and have seen what has been done to you in Egypt. And I have promised to bring you up out of your misery in Egypt'"
Exodus 3:16,17a

Read Romans 6:16.

Don't you know that when you offer yourselves to someone to obey him as slaves, you are slaves to the one whom you obey— whether you are slaves to sin, which leads to death, or to obedience, which leads to righteousness? Romans 6:16

Of what do the Israelite slaves remind us?

_____

To what were we slaves before we trusted Jesus? _____

But God had a plan to rescue the Israelites. He sent ten plagues (troubles) to the Egyptians until Pharaoh would release God's people. You may remember some of them-- locusts, frogs, boils, and

flies, to name a few. But Pharaoh was stubborn and would not let them go. We will begin the story just before the tenth plague where God gave Moses some commands for the Israelite slaves to obey. You can read those commands in Exodus 12:1-11.

> The LORD said to Moses and Aaron in Egypt, "This month is to be for you the first month, the first month of your year. Tell the whole community of Israel that on the tenth day of this month each man is to take a lamb for his family, one for each household. ... The animals you choose must be year-old males without defect, and you may take them from the sheep or the goats. Take care of them until the fourteenth day of the month, when all the people of the community of Israel must slaughter them at twilight. Then they are to take some of the blood and put it on the sides and tops of the door frames of the houses where they eat the lambs. That same night they are to eat the meat roasted over the fire, along with bitter herbs, and bread made without yeast. Do not eat the meat raw or

cooked in water, but roast it over the fire--head, legs and inner parts. Do not leave any of it till morning; if some is left till morning, you must burn it. This is how you are to eat it: with your cloak tucked into your belt, your sandals on your feet and your staff in your hand. Eat it in haste; it is the LORD's Passover."

Exodus 12:1-11

This sounds like a lot of rules to follow, doesn't it? But God has some very special things to say in each of these commands, as we will soon see. But first, let's read the most special part of this Passover story: what God did for His people!

"On that same night I will pass through Egypt and strike down every firstborn-- both men and animals-- and I will bring judgment on all the gods of Egypt. I am the LORD. The blood will be a sign for you on the houses where you are; and when I see the blood, I will pass over you. No destructive plague will touch you when I strike Egypt."

Exodus 12:12,13

What was sacrificed to save the Israelites?_____
So Moses and the people followed all the instructions God gave them. And here is what God did for them!

At midnight the LORD struck down all the firstborn in Egypt, from the firstborn of Pharaoh, who sat on the throne, to the firstborn of the

The Lord's Supper... Let's Get Ready!

prisoner, who was in the dungeon, and the firstborn of all the livestock as well. Pharaoh and all his officials and all the Egyptians got up during the night, and there was loud wailing in Egypt, for there was not a house without someone dead.

During the night Pharaoh summoned Moses and Aaron and said, "Up! Leave my people, you and the Israelites! Go, worship the LORD as you have requested. Take your flocks and herds, as you have said, and go. And also bless me." Exodus 12:29-32

The blood on the doorposts protected God's chosen people when the Egyptians were judged for their sin. They were "passed over" in judgment (hence the name "Passover") and rescued from slavery. Now the Israelites were finally free! What a celebration for them that must have been!

Christ -- Our Passover Lamb!

Now for the good part! What does this all mean for me?
Read 1 Corinthians 5:7b.

For Christ, our Passover lamb, has been sacrificed.
1 Corinthians 5:7b

Who is being compared to the lamb in the Passover story? _____

How were the Jews "passed over" in the book of Exodus?

_____

_____

Why do you think Jesus is called the Passover Lamb?

_____

_____

_____

Next week we will look at that Passover night when Jesus gave the first communion and see what it means for us!

For Next Week:

Memorize:

Don't you know that when you offer yourselves to someone to obey him as slaves, you are slaves to the one whom you obey—whether you are slaves to sin, which leads to death, or to obedience, which leads to righteousness? Romans 6:16

Read:

Luke 22 (whole chapter)

Don't forget to review this week's session!!

Communion ~
Where Did It All Begin Anyway?

ACROSS

3. Sharing in Christ with each other

4. Our big and bad problem

5. Adam and Eve ___ God

8. Our relationship to sin without Jesus

11. Sin ___ us from God

12. Deep-seated hatred in Gen. 3:15

13. Those living before Jesus look ____

DOWN

1. Having in common, fellowship or sharing

2. Jesus took our ___ on the cross

4. An object that helps us understand

6. Our Passover ___

7. God ___ the Israelites from slavery

9. ___ entered the world because of sin

10. A Jewish celebration

14. Who has sinned?

Session 1
Who is Jesus?

Below are five words of a sentence. Follow the directions for each of the words, then unscramble the remaining letters in each word for a special message.

Word 1.   O U E S S J B P

Word 1 directions: Cross out the second, fifteenth, and sixteenth **letters** of the alphabet.

Unscrambled: ____ ____ ____ ____ ____

Word 2.   A S I E

Word 2 directions: Cross out the first two **vowels** in the alphabet.

Unscrambled: ____ ____

Word 3.   G R O P U T

Word 3 directions: Cross out all the **consonants** found in the word "Egypt."

Unscrambled: ____ ____ ____

Word 4.   S P E L L S C A R V O G

Word 4 directions: Cross out the third, seventh, and twelfth **letters** of the alphabet.

Unscrambled: ____ ____ ____ ____ ____ ____ ____

Word 5.   D E A L M B O X

Word 4 directions: Cross out all the **letters** found in the word "Exodus."

Unscrambled ____ ____ ____ ____

ABCDEFGHIJKLMNOPQRSTUVWXYZ

The Message:

_____

____   _____

_____   _____ .

Session 2
The Last Supper

A Gift From Jesus
On Passover

The Last Supper

The Great Miracle!

The first communion was given to Jesus' disciples when they were celebrating Passover. Passover was a great miracle for the Israelites. Pharaoh had been very stubborn and would not let them go free, even after God had sent nine plagues to the Egyptians. Can you imagine how grateful they must have been to have finally been freed from slavery after so many years? After they escaped Egypt and God brought them miraculously across the Red Sea, they sang and praised Him for rescuing them. Read Exodus 15:1.

Then Moses and the children of Israel sang this song to the LORD, and spoke, saying:

"I will sing to the LORD, For He has triumphed gloriously!"

Exodus 15:1 NKJV

God commanded them to continue to celebrate the Passover meal every year to remember how they had been freed from slavery. So every year God's people would celebrate Passover. Then, on one special Passover night, Jesus asked His disciples to gather together to eat the Passover meal with Him. In Luke 22:12, He asked them to find the room and prepare it.

Read Luke 22:12, 13.

"And he will show you a large, furnished upper room; prepare it there."
And they left and found everything just as He had told them; and they
prepared the Passover. Luke 22:12,13 NASB

That Special Night

Read Luke 22:12 again. When Jesus met with His disciples, what event were they celebrating?

_____

Meanwhile, other important things were happening. Read Luke 22:1,2 and Luke 22:54.

Now the Feast of Unleavened Bread, which is called the Passover, was
approaching. The chief priests and the scribes were seeking how they
might put Him to death; for they were afraid of the people.
Luke 22:1,2 NASB

Having arrested Him, they led Him and brought Him into the high
priest's house. Luke 22:54 NKJV

What was about to happen?

_____

Jesus had already told His disciples that this would happen, but they didn't completely understand.

"You know that after two days is the Passover, and the Son of Man will be delivered up to be crucified." Matthew 26:2 NKJV

What did He tell them?

_____

_____

_____

It was not a coincidence that the Passover meal and Jesus' arrest and death on the cross came at the same time. Last week we learned that Jesus is our Passover Lamb.

Let's read 1 Corinthians 5:7b again.

For Christ, our Passover lamb, has been sacrificed.
1 Corinthians 5:7b

Do you remember how the Jews were "passed over" when they put the blood of the lamb on their doorposts? They were protected by God from His judgment on the Egyptians. The Jews were rescued from slavery, but we are rescued from far more!

When we put our trust in Jesus, we are rescued from sin and death and "passed over" in the final judgment! Jesus is our Passover Lamb!!!

Passover Parallels Puzzle

This next section is really interesting! There are many symbols in the Old Testament Passover that can be compared to us and our relationship to Christ. We already read that Christ is our Passover Lamb. Let's see if we can figure out some more of the symbols! Re-read the Passover story verses on pages 18-20 in Session 1. Then read the following Scriptures and compare them to the Passover story you read. The first two are done for you.

Passover Parallels

OLD TESTAMENT- WHAT HAPPENED TO THE JEWS	NEW TESTAMENT SCRIPTURE	WHAT DOES IT MEAN FOR ME?
Israelites were slaves	Romans 6:16	We were slaves to sin
Passover lamb saved them from death	1 Corinthians 5:7	Christ saves us from death
Blood of the lamb on the doorposts saved them	1 Peter 1:19	
They were to choose a lamb without defect for a sacrifice	1 Peter 1:19	
The lamb was not to have a broken leg	John 19:36	
They were to prepare bread without yeast	1 Corinthians 5	
They were to have sandals on and staff in hand	Luke 12:40	
The Israelites were freed from their captors	John 8:36	

Can you see how meaningful it is that Jesus gave the first communion to His disciples on Passover night? And this is the same night that He was arrested to suffer and die in our place for our sin.

Let's look further at what happened that night. Read Luke 22:14-16 and Luke 22:19, 20.

> When the hour came, Jesus and his apostles reclined at the table. And he said to them, "I have eagerly desired to eat this Passover with you before I suffer. For I tell you, I will not eat it again until it finds fulfillment in the kingdom of God." Luke 22:14-16

> And he took bread, gave thanks and broke it, and gave it to them, saying, "This is my body given for you; do this in remembrance of me." In the same way, after the supper he took the cup, saying, "This cup is the new covenant in my blood, which is poured out for you."
> Luke 22:19,20

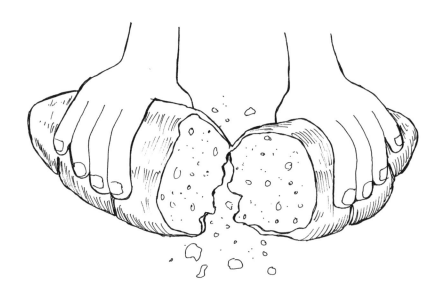

From Luke 22:19,20:

How does the bread remind us of Jesus?

_____

_____

How does the cup remind us of Jesus?

_____

_____

What are we remembering in communion?

_____

_____

_____

Jesus Shares Himself

In the first session we said that communion, in part, means sharing.
Jesus was telling the disciples that He would soon be leaving them.
He knew that He would die the next day.

Have you ever had a friend move away? There is a close bond with friends who have shared a lot together. Saying good-bye can be a very serious and caring time. If your friend were moving, you would probably want to spend some extra time together. You may want to give them something to 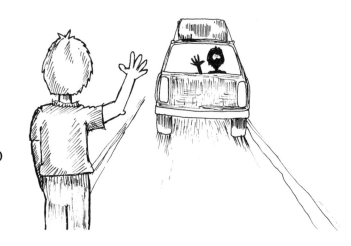 remember you by and you may even tell them "Please, don't ever forget me!"

Just like God wanted the Israelites to remember what He had done for them during Passover, Jesus wanted to give the disciples and us something so we will remember what He has done for us. Through the Lord's Supper He continues to share Himself spiritually with us, even though He is not physically here.

We certainly don't want to forget a friend, but how much more do we want to remember Jesus! He shares so much more! The Lord's Supper is a serious reminder of how He gave Himself to us in the ultimate sacrifice on the cross. He is sharing a gift that keeps on giving throughout eternity!

The Lord's Supper is very meaningful for a Christian for other reasons, too. Next session we will talk more about the importance of communion for you and me!

For Next Week:

Memorize:

Get rid of the old yeast that you may be a new batch without yeast—as you really are. For Christ, our Passover lamb, has been sacrificed.
1 Corinthians 5:7

Read:

1 Corinthians 12:18-22

Don't forget to review last week's session!!

Session 2
The First Communion

Imagine your friend told you the story of the first communion, but the room was very noisy and you weren't able to hear it very well. The story you heard did not make sense! Each of the following words rhyme with the correct word from the story on the next page. Write the correct words in the spaces that rhyme with the following words.

1. Liter

2. beware

3. can

4. mouse

5. donor

6. rode

7. plume

8. deal

9. greet

10. fable.

11. cook

12. head

13. banks

14. joke

15. Free

16. shook

17. pup

18. stew

19. flood

20. roared

21. rang

22. slim

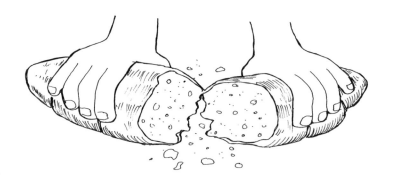

The Lord's Supper... Let's Get Ready!

The First Communion

On the day that Jesus and His disciples were going to celebrate the Passover, Jesus told _____ and John to
1
_____ the Passover meal for them. Peter and
2
John followed a _____ to a _____ and asked
3   4
the _____ where they could celebrate Passover.
5
The owner _____ them to an upper _____,
6   7
and Peter and John prepared the Passover _____
8
there. When the time came to _____ the Passover
9
meal, Jesus and His disciples reclined at the _____.
10
Jesus _____ the _____, gave _____
11   12   13
and _____ it, and said "This is My body given for
14
you; Do this in remembrance of _____." And He
15
_____ the _____ and said "This cup is the
16   17
_____ covenant in My _____, which is
18   19
_____ out for you." Then Jesus and the disciples
20
_____ a _____.
21   22

Passover Puzzle

ACROSS	DOWN
4. The last meal Jesus had with His disciples	1. God brought 10 _____ on the Egyptians
6. The bread and the cup _____ us of Jesus	2. Jesus was _____ 2 days after Passover
8. Our Passover Lamb	3. Jesus wants us to _____ Him
9. Israelites _____ praises to the Lord	5. Our Passover Lamb
10. In communion, Jesus _____ Himself	7. Lamb was to be without _____
11. Bread was to be prepared without _____	10. The cup is a _____ of Jesus' body
13. Christ saves us from _____	12. We must be _____ for Jesus return
14. God's promise to us	

The Lord's Supper... Let's Get Ready!

Session 3
What Does It Mean?

Why, What, When, Where, How?

What Does It Mean?

Have you ever played a new game that you didn't understand? Until you know all of the rules of the game, it may not make much sense and may even seem useless and silly. Until you understand the meaning of the Lord's Supper, it may not make sense to you either.   Hopefully, as you are learning more and the purpose of the Lord's Supper becomes clearer to you, it will become a very important and special part of your Christian walk!

What Is The Lord's Supper?

During the Lord's Supper we have fellowship with Jesus and other believers. When we have fellowship with Jesus we remember some very important things about Him. On the next page are three things we remember about Jesus during communion.

Read the following verses and fill in the blanks.

He himself bore our sins in his body on the tree, so that we might die to sins and live for righteousness; by his wounds you have been healed. 1 Peter 2:24

❶ During the Lord's Supper, I remember what

_____ did for me on the _____.

We are reminded of something else from the following verse:

**"And surely I am with you always, to the very end of the age."
Matthew 28:20b**

❷ During the Lord's Supper, I am reminded that _____

walks with _____ daily.

And Jesus also said:

**For whenever you eat this bread and drink this cup, you proclaim the
Lord's death until he comes. 1 Corinthians 11:26**

To His disciples He stated:

> **"I tell you, I will not drink of this fruit of the vine from now on until that**
> **day when I drink it anew with you in my Father's kingdom."**
> **Matthew 26:29**

❸ During the Lord's Supper, we remember that Jesus will return to

share in _____

with us as He did with His _____.

> **So... when we have fellowship with Jesus, we think about**
> **what Jesus did for us in the past,**
> **what He is doing for us now, and**
> **what He will do for us in the future.**

During the Lord's Supper, we also have fellowship with other
believers.   Read the following verses.

> **Because there is one loaf, we, who are many, are one body,**
> **for we all partake of the one loaf. 1 Corinthians 10:17**

> **The body is a unit, though it is made up of many parts; and though all its**
> **parts are many, they form one body. So it is with Christ. For we were all**
> **baptized by one Spirit into one body—whether Jews or Greeks, slave or**
> **free—and we were all given the one Spirit to drink. Now the body is not**

made up of one part but of many.

1 Corinthians 12:12-14

Even though we are many members, we are part of one

_____.

Though we are all different, we are all a part of the body of Christ. So what else do we think about during the Lord's Supper?

❹ During the Lord's Supper, we think about _____

_____

There are some great verses in the Bible that tell us how we can live together as the body of Christ. Read the following verses about how we are to work together.

If the foot should say, "Because I am not a hand, I do not belong to the body," it would not for that reason cease to be part of the body. And if

I'M OUTTA HERE!

the ear should say, "Because I am not an eye, I do not belong to the body," it would not for that reason cease to be part of the body. If the whole body were an eye, where would the sense of hearing be? If the whole body were an ear, where would the sense of smell be?

But in fact God has arranged the parts in the body, every one of them, just as he wanted them to be. If they were all one part, where would the body be? As it is, there are many parts, but one body. The eye cannot say to the hand, "I don't need you!" And the head cannot say to the feet, "I don't need you!" On the contrary, those parts of the body that seem to be weaker are indispensable, and the parts that we think are less honorable we treat with special honor. 1 Corinthians 12:15-23a

Do all the members of your church have the same gifts? _____
What gifts do you think God has given to you? _____
_____

What do these verses say about how should we treat others in our youth group or Sunday School classes?

_____
_____

Can you think of a time when you
treated another poorly?

_____
_____

What do these verses say about how we should treat the more

popular friends compared to the less popular?

_____

_____

God tells us more about our relationships with one another in the following verses.

so in Christ we who are many form one body, and each member belongs to all the others. **Romans 12:5**

If one part suffers, every part suffers with it; if one part is honored, every part rejoices with it. **1 Corinthians 12:26**

God wants us to _____

_____

That's right! He wants us to be happy when others are happy and to be sad with others when they are sad. God gives us another way to look at our relationships with one another.

Part Of God's Family

Read 1 John 3:1a.

How great is the love the Father has lavished on us, that we should be called children of God! And that is what we are! **1 John 3:1a**

What is your relationship to God ?

_____

If your fellow believers are children of God, what relationship does that make your fellow Christians to you (in a spiritual sense)?

_____

So, as believers, we are all a part of the family of God. Fellow Christians are your sisters and brothers. The Lord's Supper is a time of sharing with the family of God. Can you think of some good things about being in a family?

_____

_____

In God's family we care for one another, encourage one another and protect one another. In God's family we help each other grow.

Let's review. We mentioned four things we think about during the Lord's Supper. They are:

1. _____

2._____

3. _____

4. _____

The first three are what we remember about _____ and

the fourth is what we remember about _____.

Who Should Receive Communion?

In Acts 2:41,42, Peter was preaching about Jesus to a large group of people. Read about what happened.

Those who accepted his message were baptized, and about three thousand were added to their number that day. They devoted themselves to the apostles' teaching and to the fellowship, to the breaking of bread and to prayer. Acts 2:41,42

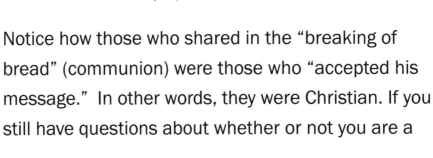

Notice how those who shared in the "breaking of bread" (communion) were those who "accepted his message." In other words, they were Christian. If you still have questions about whether or not you are a

The Lord's Supper... Let's Get Ready!

Christian, you should speak with your teacher today.

So who should receive communion? _____

Why Do We Receive The Lord's Supper?

By now you have learned a lot about the Lord's Supper and you can probably think of a lot of good reasons to receive it. Let's review some of those reasons:

_____

_____

Another reason is found in Luke 22:19,20. Read those verses.

> And he took bread, gave thanks and broke it, and gave it to them, saying, "This is my body given for you; do this in remembrance of me."
> In the same way, after the supper he took the cup, saying, "This cup is the new covenant in my blood, which is poured out for you."
> Luke 22:19,20

Circle which statement Jesus says to His disciples.

"Do this only if you want to."
"Do this."
"Don't do this."

What is another reason we should receive the Lord's Supper?

_____

Yes, because God says "do this." And we want to obey.

When Should We Receive Communion?

God doesn't tell us how often we should receive the Lord's Supper.
You may go to a church where communion is celebrated once a
month, or more or less often. The following verse doesn't stress the
time, but it does stress something else.

In the same way, after supper he took
the cup, saying, "This cup is the new
covenant in my blood; do this, whenever
you drink it, in remembrance of me."
1 Corinthians 11:25

In 1 Corinthians 11:25 Jesus doesn't stress
when to have the Lord's Supper. Instead, He says,
"Do this, *whenever* you drink it,

_____

_____."

Our focus needs to be on Jesus and not on the act itself.

Where Should We Receive The Lord's Supper?

The Bible doesn't tell us specific places to receive the Lord's Supper, But we can look at examples of believers receiving communion in the early church.   Read Acts 2:42,44.

They devoted themselves to the apostles' teaching and to the fellowship, to the breaking of bread and to prayer. All the believers were together and had everything in common. Acts 2:42,44

Here is an example of breaking of bread (receiving communion) when all the believers were

_____.

An obvious place then to receive the Lord's Supper is when you are with fellow believers in

_____.

Another example we can read in Scripture of communion is found in Acts 2:46b-47a.

They broke bread in their homes and ate together with glad and sincere hearts, praising God and enjoying the favor of all the people. Acts 2:46b-47a

Another place they shared in the Lord's Supper was in their

_____.

The Lord's Supper may also be received in the case where a person may not be able to come to church due to an illness or another cause. A pastor sometimes takes the communion to them so that they won't miss receiving it.

We have answered a lot of questions about the Lord's Supper in this session. But it is important that your heart is ready also. In the next session we will talk about how YOU can get ready for communion!

For Next Week:

Memorize:

They devoted themselves to the apostles' teaching and to the fellowship, to the breaking of bread and to prayer. All the believers were together and had everything in common.   Acts 2:42,44

Read:

Matthew 28:18-20

Mark 8:34

Mark 10:17-31

Psalm 68:3

Don't forget to review last week's session!!

Session 3
What is Communion?

Imagine your friend sent you a secret message by the sounds of a touch tone cell phone. You can tell by the tone which number on the keypad was pressed. Each of the numbers corresponds to three possible letters.

There is a number under each of the letters of the message below. Solve this puzzle by using the telephone key pad on the opposite page to choose which letter each number might stand for. Fill in the letters and decode to find the message.

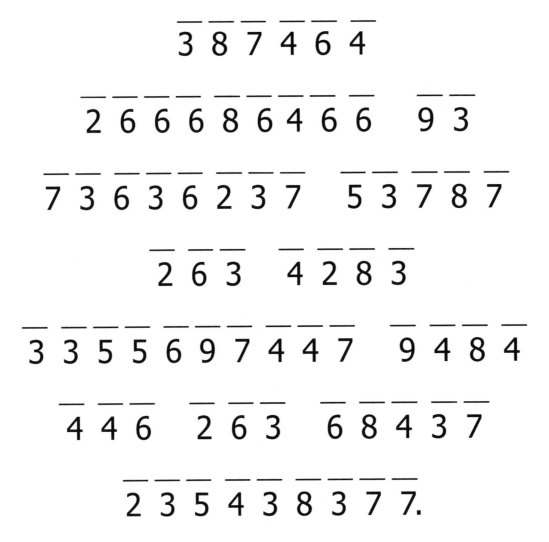

```
__ __ __ __ __ __
 3  8  7  4  6  4

__ __ __ __ __ __ __ __ __    __ __
 2  6  6  6  8  6  4  6  6     9  3

__ __ __ __ __ __ __ __    __ __ __ __ __
 7  3  6  3  6  2  3  7     5  3  7  8  7

   __ __ __    __ __ __ __
    2  6  3     4  2  8  3

__ __ __ __ __ __ __ __ __ __    __ __ __ __
 3  3  5  5  6  9  7  4  4  7     9  4  8  4

__ __ __    __ __ __    __ __ __ __ __
 4  4  6     2  6  3     6  8  4  3  7

   __ __ __ __ __ __ __ __ __
    2  3  5  4  3  8  3  7  7.
```

Secret Phone Decoder

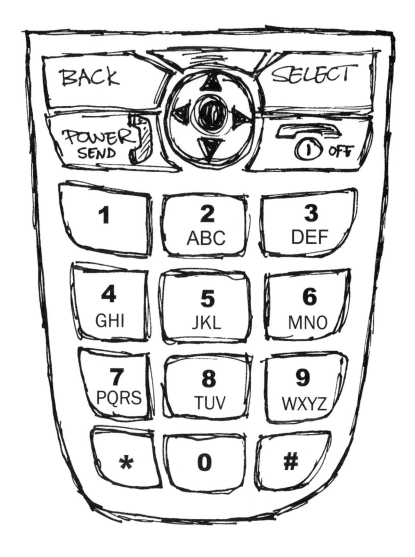

This telephone is for receiving messages only. Do not try to dial out!

Communion- My Gift

ACROSS

4. Spend time together

5. We are to ___ with each other

6. Jesus walks with me ____ day

7. The body of Christ

9. A unit, but made of many parts

11. Early believers had communion here

12. We are healed by these

13. In the Bible, some things you are good at

DOWN

1. "Do this in ___ of me."

2. Jesus gave communion first to His ___

3. Jesus will ___ to have communion with us

5. During communion we ___ what Jesus did

8. We are to ____ one another to grow

10. Also called "breaking of bread"

The Lord's Supper... Let's Get Ready!

Session 4
Getting Ready!

Doing What God Wants Me To Do

Getting Ready!

As you begin to understand more about what the Lord's Supper is, it should be increasingly more meaningful to you. God asks us to prepare our hearts before receiving the Lord's Supper. During this session we will look at the instructions God gives us that He wants us to follow before coming to communion

Our Relationship To God

Read 1 Corinthians 11:27,28

Therefore, whoever eats the bread or drinks the cup of the Lord in an unworthy manner will be guilty of sinning against the body and blood of the Lord. A man ought to examine himself before he eats of the bread and drinks of the cup. 1 Corinthians 11:27,28

As believers, we surely don't want to sin against the body and blood of the Lord. He tells us we are to _____

_____.

According to the American Heritage Dictionary, to examine means to:

observe carefully or critically; inspect, to study or analyze.

In this case, to examine means to look carefully for something within ourselves.

So what are we are to look for within ourselves?   Read 1 John 1:9.

**If we confess our sins, he is faithful and just and will forgive us our sins
and purify us from all unrighteousness.**
1 John 1:9

In order to confess our sins, we must determine that we have them.

That is the reason we must look at ourselves closely. We examine ourselves for
_____ to confess. That's right! We are to look carefully for the sin that is in us.

Only then can we ask for forgiveness. After we confess our sin and receive forgiveness, then we can truly celebrate our relationship with God!

The Main Focus

For anyone who eats and drinks without recognizing the body of the Lord eats and drinks judgment on himself. 1 Corinthians 11:29

This verse tells us we are to focus on Whom? _____

We are to recognize what He has done for us.

Read Philippians 2:8.

And being found in appearance as a man, he humbled himself and became obedient to death–even death on a cross! Philippians 2:8

What are we remembering about Christ?

_____

_____

Our Relationships With Others

Let's review what happened when you became a believer.
Read John 1:12.

Yet to all who received him, to those who believed in his name, he gave the right to become children of God. John 1:12

We learned in lesson three that as believers we are all a part of the family of God. The Lord's Supper is a time of sharing with your brothers and sisters in the family of God.

Read John 13:34,35 and look for an instruction from God.

"A new command I give you: Love one another. As I have loved you, so you must love one another. By this all men will know that you are my disciples, if you love one another." John 13:34,35

What does God command us to do in John 13:34,35?

_____

This is so important to God that He instructs us further. Read Matthew 5:23,24.

"Therefore, if you are offering your gift at the altar and there remember that your brother has something against you, leave your gift there in front of the altar. First go and be reconciled to your brother; then come and offer your gift." Matthew 5:23,24.

This verse tells us what we are to do before coming before God.

Webster's Dictionary says to reconcile means:

The Lord's Supper... Let's Get Ready!

"to restore to friendship or harmony."

According to Matthew 5, before we come before God, we are to do what? _____

Can you give an example of what this might mean in your life?

_____

_____

This concept of unity among believers is very important to God. He wants us to treat each other very well. In the following verse, circle the part that tells what you are to do with other Christians.

**If it is possible, as far as it depends on you,
live at peace with everyone. Romans 12:18**

When we come to the Lord's Supper, we are celebrating how God has given us a new relationship with Him through His forgiveness. We are celebrating how much He has forgiven us. He asks that before we come to Him, we forgive others as He has forgiven us.

God also wants us to be respectful of one another. Look at the instruction in 1 Corinthians 11:33,34.

So then, my brothers, when you come together to eat, wait for each other. If anyone is hungry, he should eat at home, so that when you meet together it may not result in judgment. 1 Corinthans 11:33,34

When we receive the Lord's Supper, we should _____ for each other. The purpose of communion is not for a snack or to satisfy hunger!

Being A Disciple Of Christ

Just as God gave the first communion to the first disciples, we also receive communion as the followers of Christ.

What does it mean to be a follower of Jesus Christ? To understand it completely, we need to look at more verses in the Bible.
Read Matthew 28:18-20.

Then Jesus came to them and said, "All authority in heaven and on earth has been given to me. Therefore go and make disciples of all nations, baptizing them in the name of the Father and of the Son and of the Holy Spirit, and teaching them to obey everything I have commanded you. And surely I am with you always, to the very end of the age."
Matthew 28:18-20

Look at the verse above and see if you can find some action words that describe what followers of Jesus do. Write them below. The first letter of each word is given.

G_____ M_____ _____

B_____ T_____ O_____

So when we are a disciple of Jesus, we will do these things ourselves and help others to do them also. Matthew 28:18-20 tells us not only to do these things, but also to bring others alongside of us. We should not only be baptized but also help others be baptized. We should not only learn about Jesus ourselves but teach others also. And we should not only obey Him ourselves, but help others obey Him as well.

How Do We Follow?

In Luke 10:27a, we read of how we are to follow Christ.

He answered: "Love the Lord your God with all your heart and with all your soul and with all your strength and with all your mind"
Luke 10:27a

We are to follow Christ with all of our _____, with all of our _____, with all of our _____ and with all of our _____.

Do you think He wants us to give Him every part of us? _____

"ALL" of our heart, soul, strength and mind means that there should be nothing more important to us than God. Think of your favorite thing to do or your favorite food or your favorite person. As much as we love those things, God should still be more important to us.

Jesus Says, "Follow Me"

Read Mark 8:34.

> **Then he called the crowd to him along with his disciples and said: "If anyone would come after me, he must deny himself and take up his cross and follow me." Mark 8:34**

What does it mean to deny yourself?

_____

What must you be willing to give up to follow Christ?

_____

In Mark 10:21, what did Jesus tell the rich young man who wanted to be a follower?

Jesus looked at him and loved him. "One thing you lack," he said. "Go, sell everything you have and give to the poor, and you will have treasure in heaven. Then come, follow me."
Mark 10:21

"I'm a living sacrifice?"
Romans 12:1

Jesus Christ won't necessarily ask you to give up everything you enjoy, but He wants to be the most important person in your life-- more important than any thing or any other person.

This does not mean that God wants us to be unhappy.

But may the righteous be glad and rejoice before God; may they be happy and joyful. Psalm 68:3

When will we be the most happy?

_____

_____

_____

God wants us to be happy in Him!

God Wants Us To Grow!

Jesus wants us to grow everyday in our relationship with Him. Below are some ways that you can be a follower of Jesus. Next to each of these, write something that you can do that you may not already be doing or can do better.

Learn more about Jesus

_____

Love Him more

_____

Serve Him

_____

Live for Him

_____

Help others to know Him

_____

Congratulations! You have made it through a long and challenging study. We pray you have grown closer to the Lord and your desire to serve Him has increased. We hope that receiving the Lord's Supper will have new meaning for you and your walk with the Lord will be productive, exciting and joyful as God teaches you more about Himself. May you continue to grow in the Lord as you love and serve Him!

But grow in the grace and knowledge of our Lord and Savior Jesus Christ.
To him be glory both now and forever! Amen. 2 Peter 3:18

For Next Week
and the Rest of your Life:

Memorize:

Scripture Regularly

Read:

The Bible Regularly

Don't forget to
review all of the sessions!!

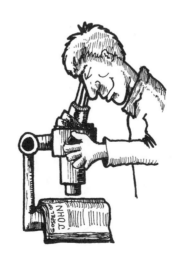

Session 4
Find the Words!

Find the following important words from all of the lessons. In the grid below, look to where the color row and the object column intersect. Use those letters to spell the word in the puzzle.

	Lamb	Bread	Cross	Cup	Staff
red	S	O	E	T	L
blue	I	D	Y	M	B
orange	N	U	J	F	W
green	V	Z	A	X	R
purple	C	K	P	H	G

1. ◯ ◯ ◯ ◯ ◯ ◯ ◯ ◯
blue-bread   blue-lamb   red-lamb   purple-lamb   blue-lamb   purple-cross   red-staff   red-cross

2. ◯ ◯ ◯ ◯
red-staff   red-bread   green-lamb   red-cross

3. ◯ ◯ ◯ ◯ ◯ ◯ ◯
purple-lamb   red-bread   orange-lamb   orange-cup   red-cross   red-lamb   red-lamb

The Lord's Supper... Let's Get Ready!

4.

◯ ◯ ◯ ◯
red-   blue-   red-   blue-
bread   staff   cross   cross

5.

◯ ◯ ◯ ◯ ◯ ◯ ◯ ◯ ◯
red-   green-   purple- green-   blue-   orange- blue-   purple- red-
lamb   cross   lamb   staff   lamb   cup   lamb   lamb   cross

6.

◯ ◯ ◯ ◯ ◯ ◯ ◯ ◯
green-   red-   blue-   red-   blue-   blue-   red-   green-
staff   cross   cup   cross   cup   staff   cross   staff

7.

◯ ◯ ◯ ◯ ◯ ◯ ◯ ◯
red-   purple- green-   orange- purple- orange- orange- red-
cup   cup   cross   lamb   bread   cup   bread   staff

I Want To Do These Things!

ACROSS	DOWN
1. Restore friendship or harmony	2. We examine sin within ___.
4. Part of the family of God	3. Inspect, study or analyze
5. Love God with ___ your heart	6. Knowing more about God
8. Will be happy and joyful	7. We need to get ___ for communion
10. We are commanded to ___ one another	9. Don't receive communion in an ___ manner
11. We focus on ___ during communion	13. We must ___ our sin
12. Follower of Jesus	
14. To be as one in some way	
15. Make clean	
16. Refuse or put something aside	

REVIEW AND BEYOND

Review and Beyond: Session 1

1. What does the Greek word "koinonia" mean?

2. According to 1 Corinthians 10:16, in what are we sharing?

3. Who gave the first communion and was that in the New or Old Testament?

4. On what special holiday did the Last Supper occur?

5. What did Passover celebrate?

6. What does Genesis 3:14 mean for you? You can review pages 13-15.

7. How were the Old Testament believers saved, since they lived before Jesus was born?

8. According to Exodus, to whom and where were the Israelites slaves?

9. When God brought judgment on the Egyptians with the tenth plague, which animal was used to rescue the Israelites? Does that have significance?

10. From what did God rescue the Israelites?

11. To what types of things can we be slaves?

12. *Bonus question: Can you find a verse in the New Testament that describes your life after Jesus rescued you from the slavery of sin?

Review and Beyond: Session 2

1. What did Passover commemorate? Is it a happy or somber remembrance?

2. When Jesus met with His disciples on Passover, what else was happening outside of their meeting place?

3. Had Jesus told the disciples that He would be crucified? What was their response?

4. Jesus is our Passover Lamb.   During what future event will we be passed over?

5. What was the importance of using a lamb without defects in Old Testament sacrifices?

6. What does yeast represent in the New Testament?

7. In the Passover instructions, what was the significance of having sandals on and staff in hand?

8. How does the bread remind us of Jesus? Explain.

9. How does the cup remind us of Jesus? Explain.

10. What is the purpose of the Old Testament sacrifices?

11. *Bonus question: Can you find a verse in the New Testament that asks us to be a sacrifice? What does it mean?

Review and Beyond: Session 3

1. During the Lord's Supper, what do we remember about Jesus that happened in the past?

2. During the Lord's Supper, what do we remember about Jesus that happens now?

3. During the Lord's Supper, what do we remember about Jesus that will happen in the future?

4. Besides Jesus, who do we have fellowship with during the Lord's Supper?

5. To whom does the "body of Christ" refer?

6. How are we supposed to treat other believers?

7. How can you help other believers in God's family grow?

8. Who should receive the Lord's Supper?

9. Does Jesus command us to receive the Lord's Supper?

10. Where did the disciples often receive communion?

11. What is a covenant?

12. What is the New Covenant that Jesus talks about in Luke 22:20?

Review and Beyond: Session 4

1. How can we "sin against the body and blood of the Lord"?

2. What does it mean to "examine ourselves"?

3. When we see sin in our lives, what must we then do?

4. Who are we to primarily focus on during communion?

5. According to John 13:35, how will men know that we are Jesus' disciples?

6. What does it mean to reconcile with your brother?

7. How can you show that you are a disciple of Christ?

8. How does a believer "deny himself and take up the cross" as instructed in Mark 8:34?

9. Do you have to give up everything you enjoy because you are a Christian?

10. When should we be the most happy?

11. What are some things you can do this week to serve God?

12. *Bonus question: Can you explain what new meaning the Lord's Supper now has for you?

Mega- Challenge

Answer this question: Where in the Bible did God first tell us that he would send Jesus to earth to solve our sin problem? Let's look at the Scripture together.

Read Genesis 3:1-15. God loves us so much that He doesn't want to see us die and be separated from Him. He wants us to live forever with Him. So right then in the Garden of Eden, He gave a promise to benefit all mankind. Read Genesis 3:15 and see what God said to Satan who was disguised as a serpent.

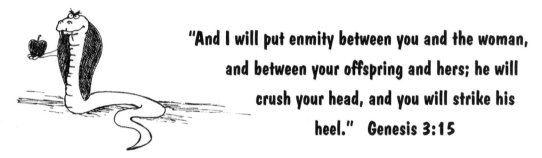

"And I will put enmity between you and the woman, and between your offspring and hers; he will crush your head, and you will strike his heel." Genesis 3:15

To whom is God talking?_____

Now let's look at who the offspring is, as described in Genesis 3:15 (hint: not Cain and Abel).

Read Galatians 4:4.

But when the time had fully come, God sent his Son, born of a woman, born under law... Galatians 4:4

Here God is promising that Jesus Christ, God's Son, would be born as a man.

Dictionary.com defines enmity as "deep-seated, often mutual ha-tred." The word enmity is a word we don't use very often, but it is like the word "enemy".

Re-read Genesis 3:15 and notice what God says to Satan, who was disguised as a serpent in verse 15. Who would be enemies? _____ and the woman and her _____

Who do you think is the offspring?

_____

Yes, the woman's offspring is Jesus.

Who strikes and bruises the offspring's heel?

_____

Who crushes the serpent's head?

_____

Genesis 3:15 tells us that Jesus (God Himself) will come as a man, and even though He is bruised as a man, He will ultimately crush the head of the enemy, Satan.

So way back in the Garden of Eden (Genesis 3:15) God first tells man about His victory plan for us.

But he was pierced for our transgressions, he was crushed for our iniqui-ties; the punishment that brought us peace was upon him, and by his wounds we are healed. Isaiah 53:5

Glossary

Amen- so it is, or so it shall be

Apostle- one whom Christ Himself chose to preach the gospel

Atonement- the restoration of relationship between God and man made possible by Jesus' death and resurrection

Blemish- a mark or area of imperfection

Carnal- worldly, sinful, corrupt

Christ- Messiah, "Anointed One"

Christian- one who believes in Jesus Christ as Lord and Savior and trusts in Him only for salvation

Communion- fellowship, the sharing of thoughts or feelings

Condemnation- punishment for sin, severe reproof

Confession- agreeing with God concerning our sin, admitting guilt

Conversion- God's act of working faith in Christ Jesus in the heart of one who does not believe

Corruptible- susceptible to depravation, subject to decay

Death- Physical death: of the body

       Spiritual death: separation from God through our refusal to trust in Jesus

       Eternal death: separation from God forever

Doctrine- teaching based on God's Word, the Bible

Eternal- has no beginning and no end

Evangelical- pertaining to the Gospel or the spreading of the Gospel

Exhort- to urge to do what is right

Everlasting- goes on forever

Faith- trust and reliance in that which you cannot see but are confident in

Fall of Man (the fall)- refers to the first act of disobedience by Adam and Eve in the Garden of Eden

Fear of God- appropriate respect and honor of God

Flesh- man's sinful nature, his inability to do what God commands

Gentile- a non-Jew

Glorify- to worship, give glory, honor or high praise to, exalt

Gospel- good news of Jesus Christ

Grace- undeserved love or favor

Holy- pure, sinless

Hypocrite- one who pretends to be something he is not

Immersion- immersing or dipping

Immutable- unchangeable, unalterable

Incarnate- Jesus Christ, who is God the Son, became man, while remaining God

Iniquity- sin, depravation

Intercession- pleading on behalf of others

Judgment- punishment, a just decision

Just- lawful, right, righteous, guiltless

Justification- God declares a sinner righteous, by counting Christ's righteousness as His

Kingdom- sphere in which a king has sovereign control

Last Supper- Passover night, when He gave His disciples the first communion

Law- commandments from God

Soul- the spiritual nature of humans

Supplication- asking for humbly or earnestly

Tempt- to test

Trespasses- those things which violate God's will

Trinity- the unfathomable nature of God being three Persons, yet one God

Truth- what God's Word teaches; sometimes Jesus Christ is referred to as the Truth

Worship- to express praise and honor, to adore

Word- God's communication to us; the Bible, or sometimes Jesus is referred to as "The Word"

wrath- God's anger against sin

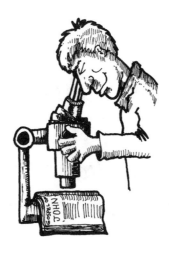

I have hidden your word in my heart that I might not sin against you.
Psalm 119:11

(BUT DON'T HIDE IT SO YOU CAN'T FIND IT AGAIN!!)

Neither do people light a lamp and put it under a bowl. Instead they put it on its stand, and it gives light to everyone in the house. Matthew 5:15

Scripture Memory

Don't you know that when you offer yourselves to someone to obey him as slaves, you are slaves to the one whom you obey—whether you are slaves to sin, which leads to death, or to obedience, which leads to righteousness? Romans 6:16

Get rid of the old yeast that you may be a new batch without yeast—as you really are. For Christ, our Passover lamb, has been sacrificed. 1 Corinthians 5:7

They devoted themselves to the apostles' teaching and to the fellowship, to the breaking of bread and to prayer. All the believers were together and had everything in common. Acts 2:42,44

But grow in the grace and knowledge of our Lord and Savior Jesus Christ. To him be glory both now and forever! Amen. 2 Peter 3:18

Endorsed by

"This is a great effort that I recommend highly for churches that desire to expose their children to solid teaching on the Lord's table. This book could be utilized in Children's Church and Sunday School, by parents, and in every area, make a significant impact for this critical matter of confession of sin and worship of our crucified, risen Lord."

John MacArthur

A Reader's Thanks

"As Child Evangelism Fellowship missionaries, we disciple children as well as evangelize them. As we disciple them to obey Christ, *The Lord's Supper... Let's Get Ready!* will be an indispensable tool. We praise our Lord for your providing this resource and for your service to Him as you prepared it."

Jerry Baccus, Missionary Director, Ventura County Chapter
Child Evangelism Fellowship

Our Thanks

Many thanks to the diligent servants who contributed in some way to this book. We are grateful for Pat Papenhausen, Lauren Donahue, and Andrea Ewing, careful readers who have refined our words and sharpened the message. Thanks to Ed at Design Loft and Jon and Josh at Design Point for their extremely artistic talent. Thanks to Scott, who by his illustrations was able to capture a lighthearted yet reverent presentation. Thank you to Kathy Burr, Cindy Pitts and Jerry Baccus for their invaluable input. Thanks to Marv, Arnold and Jean at Delta Printing.

Tim and Donna, thank you for your inspiration and support. And we give You, Jesus Christ our Lord and Savior, highest praise and gratitude for the gifts you so freely give. May we always be grateful.

Laurie Donahue and Paul Phillipps

Contributors

Paul Phillipps received his Bachelor of Arts degree at the University of Southern California (Philosophy), and his Master of Divinity (M.Div.) and Master of Theology (Th.M.) degrees at The Master's Seminary. He served as the college pastor at Grace Community Church under John MacArthur prior to the last fifteen years as a senior pastor. Husband of wife, Donna, and father of nine children, he is presently senior pastor at Pleasant Valley Baptist Church.

Laurie Donahue is the author of *God...Should I Be Baptized?* (LifeSong Publishers), *God's Plan... My Response* (LifeSong Publishers), and *A Promise Is...* (Standard Publishing). Laurie directed and choreographed children for the *In My Garden* Videos (Mary Rice Hopkins) and directed, produced and wrote music for *4-Ever His!* She holds a lifetime California Community College Teaching Credential. Laurie lives in Camarillo with her husband, Tim, and intermittently with one or two of her four, pretty-much-grown-up daughters.

Scott Palmer (internal illustrations) is an artist and illustrator who lives in San Diego. He most enjoys using the talents God has given him for the growth of His Kingdom.

Ed Olson's (cover illustration) illustration and animation career includes projects for the Walt Disney Company, Warner Brothers, Sony and Hanna-Barbera. Believing that the media can be used to reflect Christ in a relevant and respectful way to children, he has developed a design and concept development company which provides production services to Christian-based publishing and media companies. He recently directed and produced an episode of "Adventures in Odyssey" for Focus on the Family. Ed resides in Moorpark, California, with his wife and two children. Visit him at: www.websdirect.com/designloft.

Available from

LifeSong Publishers

-Baptism Preparation-

God... Should I Be Baptized?
ISBN 0-9718306-1-4
$10.99 100pp 8.5x11
For children 8-12

God's Plan... My Response
ISBN 0-9718306-0-6
$9.99 96pp 6x9
For Jr. Hi / Hi School

-Ancient Paths for Modern Women Series-

by Judy Gerry

"This is what the Lord says: 'Stand at the crossroads and look; ask for the
ancient paths, ask where the good way is, and walk in it,
and you will find rest for your souls.'"

(Jeremiah 6:16)

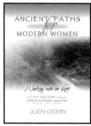

Walking With the Lord
ISBN 0-9718306-2-2
$11.99 100pp 7.5x10

Walking as Wives
ISBN 0-9718306-3-0
$11.99 112pp 7.5x10

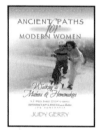

Walking as Mothers
and Homemakers
ISBN 0-9718306-4-9
$11.99 110pp 7.5x10

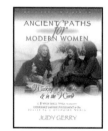

Walking in the Church
and in the World
ISBN 0-9718306-5-7
$11.99 130pp 7.5x10

"Judy Gerry has dug deeply into the sacred records of the Bible to surface divine guidance for women in every generation. Here is a timely, reassuring and professionally crafted study resource which belongs in every church library and on the study agenda for thinking women." **Howard G. Hendricks, Distinguished Professor, Dallas Theological Seminary**

"Judy… leads women to discover and apply the tried, true, and enduring way laid out for us in the Scripture- the pathway that leads to blessing and joy. In a day when so many Christian women are floundering and confused, the wisdom found in this program is timely and desperately needed." **Nancy Leigh DeMoss, Author- Host of Revive Our Hearts Radio**

Ask for these at your local
Christian Bookstore

or contact:
LifeSong Publishers
P.O. Box 183, Somis, CA 93066-0183
www.LifeSongPublishers.com
805-655-5644

-Or mail the order form on next page-

LifeSong Publishers provides additional items: gifts and rewards, 4-Ever His! music and Mary Rice Hopkins items, that may not be found in stores.

LifeSong Publishers Order Form

(See website for further description of items)

Books

	Price	Quantity	Total
God... Should I Be Baptized?	$10.99		
The Lord's Supper... Let's Get Ready!	$10.99		
God's Plan My Response	$ 9.99		
Ancient Paths 1- Walking/Lord	$11.99		
Ancient Paths 2- Walking/Wives	$11.99		
Ancient Paths 3- Walking/Mothers/Homemakers	$11.99		
Ancient Paths 4- Walking/Church/World	$11.99		
My Jelly Bean Prayer Booklet	$ 2.99		
My Busy Bible	$35.99		
Kid's Prayer Journal	$ 2.99		
Teen Prayer Journal	$ 2.99		
God's Promises To a Woman's Heart	$ 5.99		

God's Family ID Cards (no shipping on ID cards)

Silver Gold Yellow

1- God's Family ID Card	$ .99		
25 pack- God's Family ID Card	$22.28		
50 pack- God's Family ID Card	$42.08		
100 pack- God's Family ID Card	$79.20		

Gifts and Rewards

Pewter Cross Lapel Pin on Card	$ 2.50		
Pewter Heart/Nail Lapel Pin on Card	$ 2.99		
Gods Direction Pen/Bookmark	$ 3.50		
Gods Direction Pen and Paper Set	$ 4.99		
Compass Key Chain	$ 2.50		
Gospel Cross Cloth Key Chain/Card	$ 2.00		
Plant-able Seed Cross/Bookmark	$ 2.50		
My Jelly Bean Prayer Booklet	$ 2.99		
P.R.A.Y. Bookmark	$ 1.19		
Jelly Bean Gift Bag	$ 4.19		
King's Kids Gift Bag	$ 4.19		
Pewter Nail Pendant (boxed)	$ 5.99		
Mustard Seed Pocket Coin	$ 2.00		
God Bless America Pen	$ 3.50		
God Bless America Bracelet	$ 1.00		
Rosewood Pen and Case- Appreciation Gift	$18.00		
Rosewood Pen and Case- Graduation Gift	$18.00		
Mother's Heart Cross/Heart Pin	$ 2.50		
Bouquet of Blessing Pen/Bookmark	$ 3.50		
Easter Gift Bag- Pen, Magnet, Bookmark	$ 4.99		
Iris or God's Direction Thermal Mug (circle)	$ 7.99		

4-Ever His!

4-Ever His! Cassette (discounted)	$ .99		
4-Ever His CD (discounted)	$7.99		

Mary Rice Hopkins

Mary Rice Hopkins and Co CD	$14.99		
Sing Through The Year	$14.99		
ABC's of Praise	$14.99		
Mary Rice Hopkins and Co Songbook	$14.99		
In My Garden CD	$14.99		
In My Garden Songbook	$ 5.99		
In My Garden Fruit of the Spirit Video	$10.00		
In My Garden DVD	$20.00		
In My Garden Hand Motion Learning Video	$14.99		
Mary Christmas CD	$14.99		
Mary Christmas Songbook	$14.99		
Lullaby CD	$14.99		
Lighthouse CD	$14.99		
Come On Home Parables CD	$14.99		
Miracle Mud CD	$14.99		
Juggling Mom CD	$14.99		
Whispering Wind (Adult) CD	$14.99		
In the Beginning	$14.99		
If I Knew How to Moo	$14.99		
Canciones Para Toda La Familia	$14.99		

Subtotal of all Columns _____

CA Sales Tax (CA Residents Only) 7.25% of subtotal _____

Shipping Media Mail $3.00 or $4.00 for over 3 items (7-10 days)

Shipping Priority 7% of total/minimum of $5.00 (3-4 days)

Total _____

Name and/or Church _____

Address _____

City, State, Zip _____

Phone (   ) _____

Email _____

This address is my ____ Church ____ Home ____ Other

Make check payable to:

Lifesong Publishers
P.O. Box 183, Somis, CA 93066-0183
Phone: 805-655-5644
www.LifeSongPublishers.com
Email: mailbox@lifesongpublishers.com

To pay by credit card: ____ Mastercard ____ Visa

Please fill out above address information

Card # _____

Exp. Date _____

Name on Card _____

Answer Key

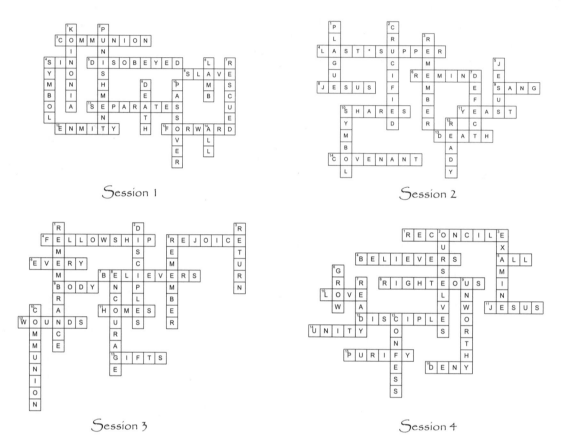

Session 1

Session 2

Session 3

Session 4

Word Puzzles

Session 1: Jesus is our Passover Lamb

Session 2:

On the day that Jesus and His disciples were going to celebrate the Passover, Jesus told **Peter** and John to **prepare** the Passover meal for them. Peter and John followed a **man** to a house and asked the **owner** where they could celebrate Passover. The owner **showed** them to an upper **room**, and Peter and John prepared the Passover **meal** there. When the time came to **eat** the Passover meal, Jesus and His disciples reclined at the **table**. Jesus **took** the **bread**, gave thanks and **broke** it, and said "This is My body given for you; Do this in remembrance of **Me**." And He **took** the **cup** and said "This cup is the **new** covenant in My **blood**, which is **poured** out for you." Then Jesus and the disciples **sang** a **hymn**.

Session 3: During communion we remember Jesus and have fellowship with Him and other believers

Session 4:
1. disiciple	5. sacrifice
2. love	6. remember
3. confess	7. thankful
4. obey	

The Lord's Supper... Let's Get Ready!